Scryptic
Magazine of Alternative Art

Issue 1.1

ISBN-13: 978-1548222772

ISBN-10: 1548222771

© 2017 by Stephen Chase Gagnon and Lori A Minor

Note from the Editors

Before I go any further, we would like to sincerely thank everyone who trusted us enough to send their work to Scryptic. Being artists ourselves, we both know how easy it is to be skeptical of a new journal. Especially one whose goal is to publish only the darkest work it can find. Since the birth of Scryptic, we envisioned this magazine to be a safe place for writers and artists who draw their inspiration from the darker slices of life. We all know it's been a struggle to find venues that want to showcase our words and images, but we hope to keep those days far behind us with the launch of this magazine. So please keep sending us your twisted tales, your hellish haiku, your sinful sonnets, and any other piece that feels trapped on the island of misfit art – they have a home!

We hope you enjoy reading this inaugural issue half as much as we enjoyed putting it together. We can't wait to get started on issue 1.2!

-Scryptic Editors Chase Gagnon and Lori A Minor

Table of Contents

4	Steve Hodge
5	Julie Bloss Kelsey
6-7	Kath Abela Wilson
8-12	Alexis Rotella
13	Eleanor DS
14-15	David J Kelly
16	Gunnar Bates
17	Gabriel Bates
18-19	Salil Chaturvedi
20-22	Olivier Schopfer
23	Dave Read
24-28	Mac Greene
29-31	Elliot Nicely
32-33	David Terelinck
34-38	Kyle Hemmings
39	Tiffany Shaw-Diaz
40-41	A.J. Binash
42	Mary Pagans
43	Savanna Gregory
44	Debbi Antebi
45-46	Clayton Beach
47	Margaret Jones Whitewater
48-52	Barabara Kaufmann
53	Marshall Bood
54	Carol Judkins
55-56	Marianne Paul
57	Willie R. Bongcaron
58-59	Paul Brookes
60-62	Ashley Parker Owens
63	Rachel Sutcliffe
64-65	Glen Armstrong
66	Pat Geyer
67	M.C.T.
68-71	Michael Rehling
72	Roman Lyakhovetsky
73	Deborah P. Kolodji
74	Charlotte Riewestahl
75-76	Mandy Macdonald
77-79	Leslie Bamford
80	Carol Judkins & David Terelinck
81	Brendan McBreen
82	José Angel Araguz
83-84	A.D. Adams
85-86	Jerry Dreesen
87	Susan Burch
88	Tracy Davidson
89-90	Annika Lindok
91	Angelica Costantini-Hartl
92	Tyson West
93	Robert Kingston
94-95	Angelo B. Ancheta
96-98	Toti O'Brien
99	Jim Lewis
100-102	Kathleen A. Lawrence
103-104	Roger Leege
105	Bob Bamford
106	Marion Clarke
107-109	Jake Cosmos Aller
110-111	Darrell Lindsey
112	Kris Moon
113-114	Shanna Baldwin-Moore
115	RP Verlaine
116	David Terelinck
117-119	Susan Mallernee
120-123	Richard Stevenson
124	Book Review *The Black Between Stars*
125-127	Lori A Minor
128-130	Chase Gagnon

Night Shift

The girl is watching a beetle climb up her bedroom window. It's almost to the top - to the spot where she's seen it fall twice before. She hates that her mother is working the night shift. Hates the quiet that fills the house. The beetle falls. Starts up the window again. She hears her father's footsteps in the hall. Reaches out. Crushes the bug. Her bedroom door opens. A single tear. She feels his hands on her before he touches her.

midnight clouds
no one sees the shooting star
go dark

-Steve Hodge

crime scene tape --
the puzzle piece
edged in blood

every morning
his hands tight
around my neck

driving past
the trauma unit
wishing
I could drop off
my inner child

-Julie Bloss Kelsey

last night I woke on the train to Auschwitz

unbelievable you say but it's the time
for dreams like this

all that innocence and promise
beauty and trust as if nothing worse
could ever happen

Vanishing Point

Sometimes unseen until later, but all the lines start there.
Look for it, he says.
I think it's in the garage. I point to a dark spot.
Close, he says, but a little to the left, and darker.
Is it bamboo or willow that overhangs the moment?
A light goes on behind a stack of boxes.

a pale blue
door
opens outward
the fallen sky
is held up by clouds

Cassandra

I see the future in your eyes, deviled eggs, sun gold waxing moons. Within them time grows evergreen. I carry my heart, a locket, a seahorse. Its complicated channels, veins, arteries, all in all, my heart like an old pencil eraser. Your face a slot machine, I drop my tongue perfectly into your paused mouth.

I wait
for words
a little brush
sweeps them
away

The Stinging

This autumn day
in paradise
the bract hearth
flames bright orange.
Its blue tongue
licks toward the sky
pointing out the mystery.

I'm stung
with premonitions.
The long stemmed past
vulnerable and covered over
at its roots
forgets itself and the

buzz

of intense tomorrows
in a swarm, surrounds me
in my watery bed,
heats me up,
and the smoke has the scent of ashes.

I've my blue sheets pulled over
up to my chin as I
float in my today
knowing that
the other days
will be, and
after the stinging
they'll drop,
all of them,

one by one and float on the surface here
beside me until

we disappear.

-*Kath Abela Wilson*

-Alexis Rotella

-*Alexis Rotella*

-Alexis Rotella

-Alexis Rotella

-*Alexis Rotella*

Pyre

Mother sharpens stakes in the little kitchen. Outside, father and daughter rake leaves, leaving no corner of the garden unswept. The little girl's nose is pink from the cold, her eyes from crying. There is no curly-haired little brother this year to play pretend and bring the dead leaves back to life.

Autumn's pyre is ready. Petrol and a match turn it into a beacon to Winter that it's victory is assured.
"Do you remember how much he loved bonfires?" her father asks. She nods, knowing she will never forget. "It's a big one this year, he'd approve if he could see it."
The mother brings the stakes and apples outside.

I watch them from a window, open to let the sounds and smoke and bitter wind inside. Fools. He is watching the bonfire although they do not know it. Under the cloying leaves his little lidless eyes are open, staring upwards after eddying sparks which climb but tumble back to earth. His ashes mix with the sizzling juice of apples. Soon I will be safe.

-Eleanor DS

blood orange
weeping from
the fresh cut flesh

nudity

You ask me to undress.
With reluctance, I oblige,
slipping out of urbanity and
culture, respect and rapport.
Encouraged by the twin frissons
of shock and delight, it is easier
to carry on. There goes dignity,
morality, empathy and remorse.
Waking, alone, in a ragged remnant
of myself, I try not to remember.

heart-quake
realising the monster
isn't under the bed

What doesn't kill you ...

I was tall during my teens; taller than my friends. It helped when I wanted to buy cigarettes or alcohol. No-one asked for ID. I can't be sure, but I think that was when I mastered the art of deceit.
Lying became addictive, compulsory even. On reflection, that's probably when I also started lying to myself and the dissociation began. Life is peculiarly confusing when you lose touch with yourself. "How are you?" The question stops making sense, even if you wake up attached to a heart monitor.

self-medication
going back to the doctor
to apologise

-David J Kelly

-David J Kelly

we are
in a channel
between time and space
after nothing
and before everything

Don't strain yourself
reading
into my head

-Gunnar Bates

on the side
of an old garage
some red crayon
graffiti reads
"I Love You"

woodsmoke
sometimes I miss myself

passing by

a group of
young black men

the police car starts
slowing down
at the sight of them

cold starlight
I think of all the poets
before me

-Gabriel Bates

Last night I sat down to thank the Universe

Last night I sat down to thank the Universe
  and there was no one with me
    except my glass of whiskey and Ry Cooder
I slided down great big rivers of tunes
  to the rhythm of Ry's guitar
I flowed down valleys of notes comfortably
There was no jaggedness
  though there was pain and hope around every bar.
I kept drinking and thanking
  and sliding and thanking
  and thanking and sliding and drinking
Because there were children in slums
  and they had smiles on their faces
  and I thanked the Universe for those happy traces;
There were people who had lost loved ones
  and they were sitting in lonely corners
  salted memories washing down their cheeks
  and I thanked the Universe for those memories;
And there were shattered hearts sitting up in balconies at nights
  drawing solace from those tiny lights
  sometimes for hours
and I thanked the Universe for the lovely stars;
And there were soldiers waiting at a station
  waiting for their trains back home to familiar lanes
  waiting to substitute a soft waist for a nation
  and I thanked the Universe for those trains;
And I thanked the Universe for the night and prostitutes
And redemption and parole and for a second chance
  For Buddha and his loving trance
  For parents' belief in you
  and for the telephones they call you on.
Yes, I was thanking the Universe
  because there are lovers who meet secretly in parks
  and pull into dark spaces for long kisses
  and I thanked the Universe for love and the dark;
And there are babies, children, brothers, sisters, sons and mothers who are
  being bombarded day after day in war zones that are expanding
  and I thanked the Universe for instant deaths.
I was thanking the Universe for all this
and there was no one with me
except my glass of whiskey and Ry Cooder.

-Salil Chaturvedi

OWLS

She moves her feet away from the light, across its oval edge and into the anonymous comfort of darkness, but, it's of no use. She has a little light all her own and her shins glow in the dark.

If someone were to pass the gate and look towards her she will be seen, so she covers her face with her hands. Her milky white breasts are flattened on her thighs as she sits crouched on the front steps of the house, her forehead touching her knees in an attempt to cover herself with her own body.
She hears footsteps and shuts her eyes tighter. She follows the footsteps as they pass the gate and tick-tock away, finally being swallowed by the sound of crickets. She shivers and draws her feet closer.

The toes of her left foot clamber over the right foot, giving and seeking assurance at the same time. For a moment she feels the weight of the sky and thinks she is going to collapse under it. A chill runs down her naked spine. She can hear the children sobbing in the room. They will not come to the window to look at her sitting stark naked in front of the house.

She hears a soft rustle. She lifts her head slightly and looks through her fingers. She sees a large white owl on the wire that brings the television images into the house. The owl is looking directly at her. The owl moves its head up and down, then flies and settles on the gate to get a squarer look at her.
The door opens behind her. A shaft of yellow light races towards her, climbing her hips at an angle from the right and settles in her pubic hair.

'Are you sorry?' he says. 'If you say sorry, you can come back in and wear your clothes.'

'Otherwise?' she looks up at him defiantly.

She thinks about the owl for many days after that. At the office, people are astonished at the owls she draws during lunch breaks.

-Salil Chaturvedi

-Olivier Schopfer

-Olivier Schopfer

-*Olivier Schopfer*

visiting hours
come to an end
a crow peeks
in the window

the first
mound of dirt
hits the casket -
a Rorschach print
of unanswered prayers

last call
a drunk staggers into
my headlights

gathering clouds
the dog's cancer
fills the house

-Dave Read

Where I Broke my Head

visions in the doorway,
in the design of a carpet, the pattern of a wooden door,
the shadows of trees, the shadows of grassy weeds

that teenager is always in a bush, creeping
probably smoking weeds in a corn cob pipe
out behind the barn with the other ghosts.
that pirate in the trees, obviously not real.
that brown shadow in the ceiling, that's blood dripping slowly,
slowly dripping down from a murder in the attic.

my dog can read my mind, all my mean and dirty thoughts,
so now I'm only thinking in Albanian.
the birds are talking in their secret languages
but the wren can't understand the vireo.
they carry messages
and lead the long way through the dark forest.
there's a puzzle to solve,
17 DOWN eludes me. "rotten to the core?" starts with D?

Death is no longer in his corner.
he's dragging his crippled legs,
snuffling and scraping along the floorboard.
he's gathering up his mouse army
and his bloodsucking mosquitoes,
but I won't touch the bastard.
that's his nasty little trick,
hold his hand and he will never let you go.
the coyote trotting down the edge of my yard,
with yellow fur and flashing yellow eyes,
if he catches me in the garden
he'll call the others.
it'll be a bloody mess.

unless it's in the attic, dripping through the ceiling.
if I'm dead up there,
then I don't have to worry about Death down here.
I can cuss at him and call him names.
I'll go with the teenager
to the sparrow party in the squawking bush.

the pirate in the trees is not real.
I'm not so sure about Death.

coyotes are real and so am I.
there's someone behind my left shoulder.
do you hear my mother's voice?
she's the snarling one with yellow eyes
singing happy birthday out of tune.

I could tell you more, but the important parts are Classified.
maybe you're the one who knows
me, and knows the limits of a happy song.
the warbling vireo is happy,
so God-damned happy I can't think.
it mocks me all day, every day,
and now the sinkhole is opening.
hear the dwarves chanting?
but that's a different story
and I'm not going to tell you.

-Mac Greene

Confessional Surrealism

On a rush hour bus ride in 1972, I
argued in my head against the War
with my deadbeat military Dad,
knowing all along that the argument
was about something else, more like
abandonment than engagement.
I read once that constipation
in your 40's predicts a stroke
in your 70's, but maybe this is
metaphorical, not scatological.
I'm being phenomenological
as dog turds float down the river
of my life which due to inadequate
Federal regulation is being used as an
open sewer by all the towns upstream,
polluting my stream of consciousness
with frisky nymph orgies and industrial
chemicals which the toxicologists
classify as endocrine disruptors,
which really means life disruptors,
which is why there are 5-legged
frogs and a preponderance of female
crocodiles, and a booming porn industry
with 1000's of young men and women
eager to get paid to be laid in public,
which will probably not disrupt
private diatribes with their parents,
or re-equilibrate the crocodiles.

-Mac Greene

Be wild Be wildered
a word salad

Blink the light, sprite.
   Fade the familiar, raise the shadow,
famish the squeamish.

gleamish metal boxes,   shapely,   colory,   all wondrously,
awestruckily.
    Broken heads float   luckily.
    Ears   mouths   cigarettes appear
in the rear
view mirror.
    Fingers hang from steering wheels.
Steals through red lights fastly,   faintly   quaintly   saintly
    "I'm not feeling your charisma."
"Good, God!"   goody, goody   gumdrop

plop
rain pizzles on driveway.
    What's cookin?
    Egg   fried, sizzles with bacon,
        tried twizzlers,
knuckles knuckled up
       drink frizzlers, frizzers, fitzers on the fritzers
        "You have to break some eggheads."
     Cook, cookie cookie kooo,
coocoookerooo
I am the eggman, the cuckoo,

    the cuckold
in the sheepfold   baa baa bumble
rumble to the ritual   to the slaughter   share the bloodfeast
beast of the deep dark swamp
pomp and circumstance
debutante   celebrity ahhhnt
A sea of red fire ants
      does not enhance
        social security
      helps if you get tongue-tied
or too shy
to get your words out.

   birds out
     in the rain.   Let the wet cat out

and in and out and
           indecisive, derisive.
thunder divisive, raining, pouring, old man snoring,
bumped head, went to bed, didn't get up
in the morning, lost his mooring
           mind untethered, loosely feathered.
               Deadered
and
gone.
gone.
gone.

-Mac Greene

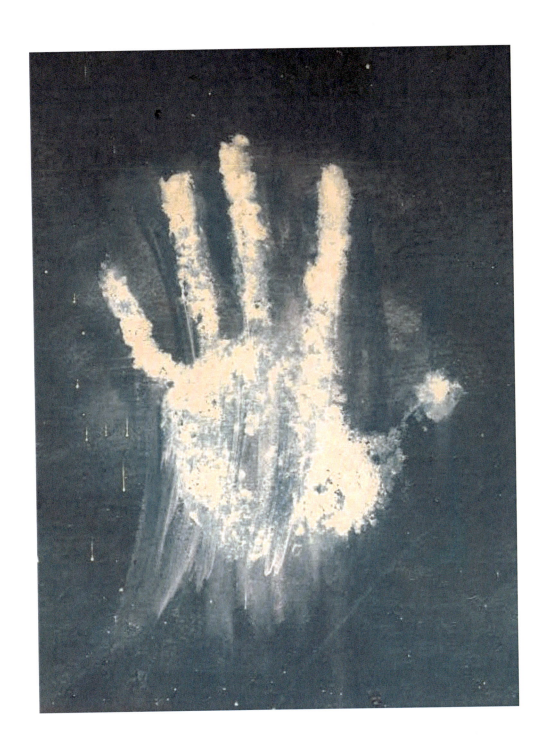

-Elliot Nicely

The Creeping Night

Black,
No room for light.
No animal dares roam
On a night like tonight.

No eyes in the bushes,
Not a sound to be heard.
And it's all around me;
I dare not say a word.

The fog is creeping in
while cold drizzle trickles down.
My mind grows uneasy,
And my heart begins to pound.

The moon's gone forever;
It has been erased.
No stars are found either;
They won't show their face.

Walking toward my home,
I keep a quick step.
But if I'll make it,
I wouldn't place a bet.

My house is just ahead,
But there's no sense of cheer;
Since the faster I walk,
The closer it draws near.

Quickly down the driveway,
No need for me to check,
It's right behind me now;
its breath upon my neck.

Skipping up the steps,
I don't turn my head.
For I know my fate:
I'll not see my bed.

A hand on the knob,
A snap of the wrist,
In one, quick motion,

Diving with a twist.

Slamming the door shut
(Now safely inside)
And in my mom's arms,
I bid Night goodbye!

-*Elliot Nicely*

Dismembered

Eyes, insubstantial in inky shadows, glance up at the sound of movement on the steps. Arthritically, the feet appear. Now legs, encased in white-ribbed orthopaedic stockings, protruding from cheap slip-ons. Eyes notice everything, registering details.

Plump and vulnerable, the body appears. Callused hands, spider-webbed with thinning veins, tightly clutch a handbag to the corpulent abdomen. Eyes come to rest on the bag. Blue. Dark blue. Pensioner blue.

Eyes see a face, lined with furrows, materializing in the unsympathetic naked light. The eyes dart quickly, returning to the bag.

The desolate cry of the locomotive ruthlessly jerks the eyes towards the tunnel. A dim glow of light flickers in the distance and builds to a constant blaze. It billows out, exploding from the tunnel as the train slices through the night, cleanly dissecting the platforms. Light splashes across everything, betraying those taking anonymous refuge in shadows.

Hot flashes of colour scorch everything. Eyes take refuge behind cheap shades of dubious ownership.

Hands adjust shades and gently massage the throbbing temple. Tapering fingers knead the creviced brow. Darting back and forth across the receding hairline, fingers continue to dismiss the pain.

Fingers curl and uncurl like cats' claws. Hands meet, fingers interlocking, forming a bridge. Collapsing. Incomplete without the right index finger. The left hand massages the stump, bereaving the loss of a loved one.

Fingers scratch at scars on the backs of hands, tracing their origins, picking at the accumulation of dirt on emaciated knuckles. Nails, chewed to the quick by yellowed fangs, tease the edges of the numerous scabs coating the hands.

The right hand feels down the leg, searching, stopping at the dilapidated boots. Gradually it withdraws the blade. Fondles. Then quickly returns it to the booted scabbard. Before retreating to the safety of pockets, the hand rubs a bruise on the lower calf.

Weight shifts from right leg to left. Feet shuffle continually. Cold steel caresses the calf, compensating for the pain of the bruise.

Ragged denims hide the scars of fights and back alley brawls. The rough cloth flaps harshly against the cadaverous legs in the artificial squall of the train.

Feet oil-slick into motion, insinuating their way out of the comfort of shadows. They slither across the platform and make for the nearest carriage. Sliding into a seat, they kick a discarded Coke bottle.

Ears listen intently as it spins to stop, concentrate on the gaggle of late night commuters. The whoosh of automatic doors kills platform noise.

Ears detect voices. Sounds of teenage laughter assault. Ears try to block out all distractions.

Eyes scan the carriage, locating the bag. The plump and vulnerable body turns around. Eyes quickly swivel. The darkness outside turns the window into a mirror. Eyes peer into their own image, seeing nothing.

Ears carefully monitor departures as successive stations take their toll of commuters.

Eyes register movement as the bag departs down the aisle. The carriage stops and the gigantic maw opens to disgorge bag and owner.

Feet, keeping their distance, propel legs in the direction of the bag.

Ears listen as the doors close silently and the metal sanctuary slides down the rails leaving a vacuum of silence in its wake.

Eyes survey the platform and come to rest on the solitary bag. They stare into the shadows again, searching. All that is seen is opportunity.

Legs become animated, moving faster. Fingers contract, curl and uncurl, flexing, feeling strong. Ears try to discern threatening noises. All that is audible is silence.

All tense, waiting. The bag opens. Ears detect sounds of a search for the ticket.

Legs propel rapidly as the right hand snakes down the leg and contacts the blade.

Feet shamble down the steps.

Eyes survey the night, seeing no one.

Hands smear crimson on torn denim.

Ears listen to the music of rain on the roof and the jingle of coins in the pocket.

The thin mouth, disappearing into darkness, breaks into a half smile.

-David Terelinck

-Kyle Hemmings

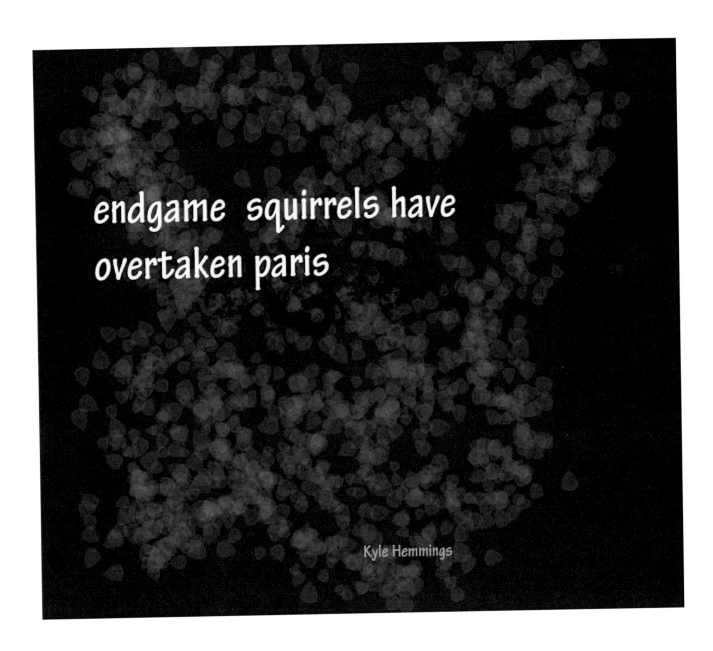

-Kyle Hemmings

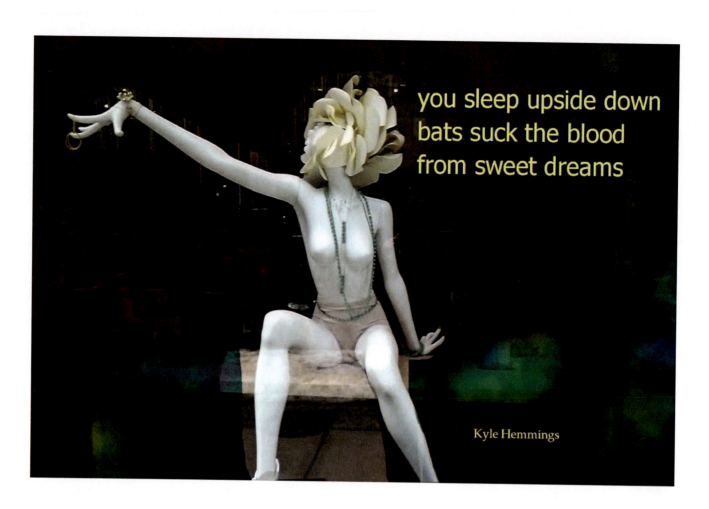

-Kyle Hemmings

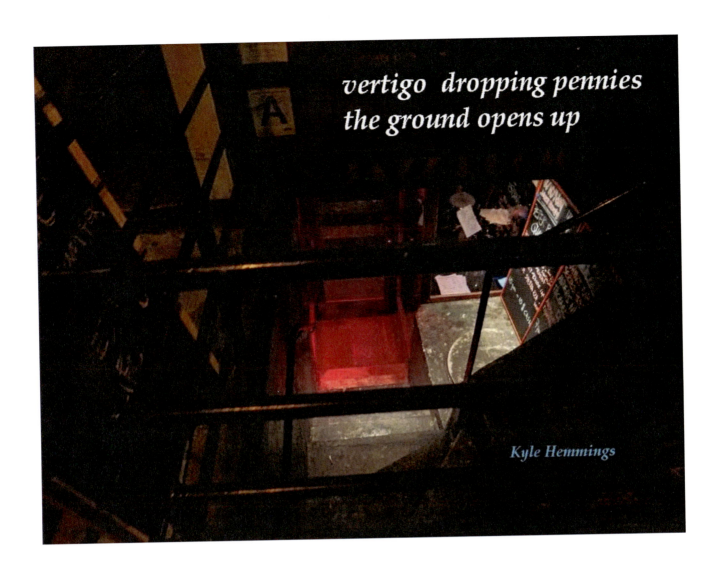

-Kyle Hemmings

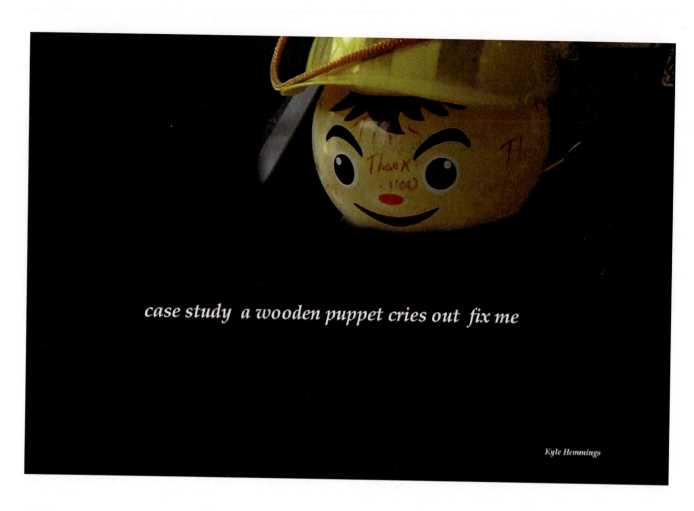

-Kyle Hemmings

up my spine
icy fingers pluck
phantom strings

bitter wind
one vulture circles
a moonless void

doomsday clock
the rhythmic scrape
of death's scythe

-Tiffany Shaw-Diaz

Guaranteed Masochism

Gaia's teeth are rotten
Even plaque
Abandoned
'em

-if what we squander
Defines us-

It's apparent
That some spend their entire existence
Becoming what they were.

Toothpicks to trees
Adults to abortions
Compliments to desires

But empty smiles
Complete a frame
Around graffiti. And to
The commonwealth
It's art
And to a bias
It's vandalism.

But to Gaia
It's her World.

-A.J. Binash

Place The Artist In A Guillotine And Kill Them Properly

Searching for a lip-less lush
When approaches the hush
Of permanent semantics.

I refrain from tattoos on collar bones,
Instead defeat acrylic paint
By watering down the canvas
With cat guts. Art sings this way,

Alone.

With a wooden string vengeance.
Brush strokes collapse
Like the fat-lady's-crescendo.

But from underneath the belly's shadow
Peaks the misbirth
Wide eyed and full of mirth.
It tip toes to the edge of the stage
And bows
A proper rehearsal of submission.

"I said plain language!"
A reverberation of fury
Exclaims the audience.

Creates standing room ONLY
For those applauding,
Winking,
Fucking off the compliments
And social cues.

We have the perfect hue
Of mute
Of leather
Of sigh. Whatever strips the flesh
From bone and positions
Sacrifice, properly. This is when
The where of confession
Mocks the honesty of truth.

-A.J. Binash

-Mary Pagans

Amen

You sing "hallelujah"
but the ground you're standing on is damned.
Skeletons kissed my lips,
pressing their fingers against my hips.
Ghosts whispered in my ears,
just exactly what they'd like to do to me,
hang me from the rafter and leave me to die,
but don't kid yourself,
you'll all have dry eyes,
I'm just the suicide of tomorrow's generation,
something I'm sure you've heard before,
while your daughter was jamming her fingers down her throat
in some fast food restaurant out west.
Blue diamond shaped pills
dictate my personality today...
"I think I'll be homicidal today! Oh what fun!"

and to that I say...

Amen.

-Savanna Gregory

starless night
a stranger's footsteps
become mine

red tide
the scabs I keep
peeling off

birthmark
some stains i can't
scratch out

phantom limb
mother's touch
goes missing

-*Debbi Antebi*

Caution Tape

Your mother left these items lain
on the unmade bed before she died:
a half eaten chicken tender on a television tray
& an ancient issue of People
Magazine. In the beginning, & the end
for that matter, you were in it together.
The middle part is where things
get sticky, like this horizon of buildings
that through the fog appear as
bits of garbage floating on the oilslick
bay. Oh, to sleep deeply in the ancient
fountain, or to fall limp in your vacant
arms again. A tattooed, toothless man
raps at the door, professes that adoration
was his only vice, then asks for the money
he knew was in her purse, & the jewelry box
with all its untold, sordid secrets. The past
is pressing on your cerebellum like a tumor,
stealing your equilibrium. By the time the last
box is packed & sent to charity, the missing years
are seeping into your blood as by osmosis.
The answer might seem obvious, but it's
never just so simple as signing the paper
then walking away from it all unscathed.

-Clayton Beach

Cumulonimbus

The world blinks for a moment
& hail fills all the wounds of the earth
with rock salt
                while the sun keeps shining.
The daffodils are bowed low—
petals tattered. I clip the few survivors
& put them in a vase.
                    Who was it
that had a portentous dream
the night before the call arrived?
Grandmother had sent a text
that she was going to return.

Somewhere, the corpse lies unwanted,
cold in its drawer. The ill fitting jacket
at the end of the evening that nobody
will come to claim.
                  You finger the ticket
guiltily, wanting to drop it & run like hell
as the train slides onto the cold steel slab
of the station.
                Here, the hailstones melt away
in the warm March sun,
but they have left their mark regardless
of whether the fleeting shadows
have passed from view.

-Clayton Beach

2 A.M. thunderstorm
I go outside
where it's quiet

stone in hand
lonely preacher
goes first

your war stories
I learn them by heart
while you sleep

-Margaret Jones Whitewater

Inside Out – A Haiga Sequence by Barbara Kaufmann

ghost story the night breeze brushes my face

on both sides of barbed wire soft moonlight

starlight the night people drift in and out

-Barbara Kaufmann

Saint Genet

growing up in a penal colony
romanticizing his borders
a transient, a thief
a faggot, a prisoner
who in his cells wrote
what was never meant to be read
without holding back anything ...
the triumph of coming to appreciate fully
the scent of his own shit

-*Marshall Bood*

Redux

I lie still in darkness, eyes wide open...see nothing, and hear noth...oh God, a loud buzzing...it doesn't stop. I can't stand it...the sound subsides then resumes as loud jackhammer-fast buzzing, then metallic tapping. Immobilized, drenched in sweat, I open my mouth to scream, but nothing comes out. This fear of being buried alive awakens.

pushing through
the tilled soil
yellow iris

As I settle myself into a chair after the MRI, the neurologist enters the room...shuffles papers as he clears his throat, then scripts my worst nightmare. I open my mouth to scream, but nothing comes o*ut.*

-*Carol Judkins*

-Marianne Paul

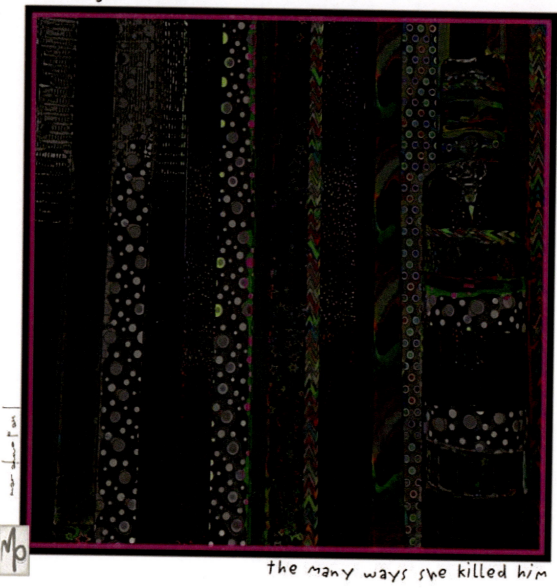

-Marianne Paul

anatomy of death
only the mangled feathers
of a dove

black cat
it is all that
a black cat

toy gun
building a camouflage
of deceit

-Willie R. Bongcaron

Clouds Are Mouths

the earth is the sole
of a giant boot
that forever presses
us into sky
as if we were insects

we cling to the grip
of the outsole
fearful of the fall
into the mouths of clouds.

Lashes Are Naked Limbs

A cold eye blinks
at the end
of the garden.

Its lashes are naked limbs
of trees, some raised
up, others reach down,
shadows of those above.

The eyeball is a loveseat
left out in a pelt of rain,
a wind moves the lashes.

-Paul Brookes

Cockroaches Skitter

This bed needs to be cold,
these sheets need to be
thin, torn and soiled.
I let fleas leach my skin.

I'm glad this bed is lumpy,
cockroaches skitter
across the rotten floorboards,
in and out damp earthquakes
of damp paint and plaster.

I am happy here

-Paul Brookes

-Ashley Parker Owens

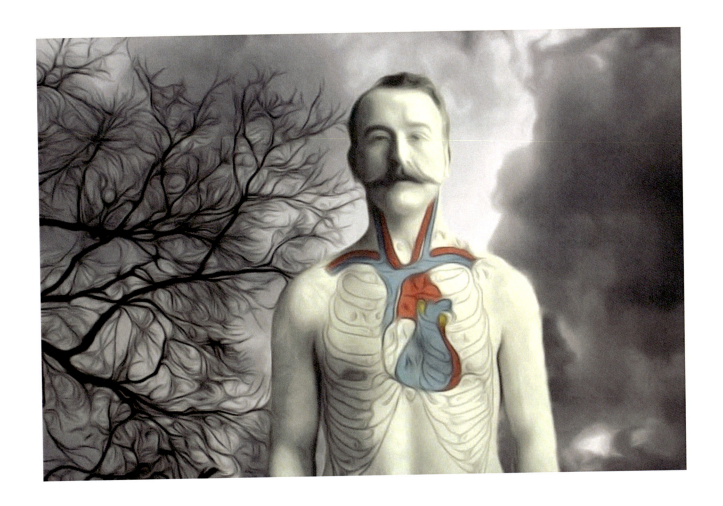

-Ashley Parker Owens

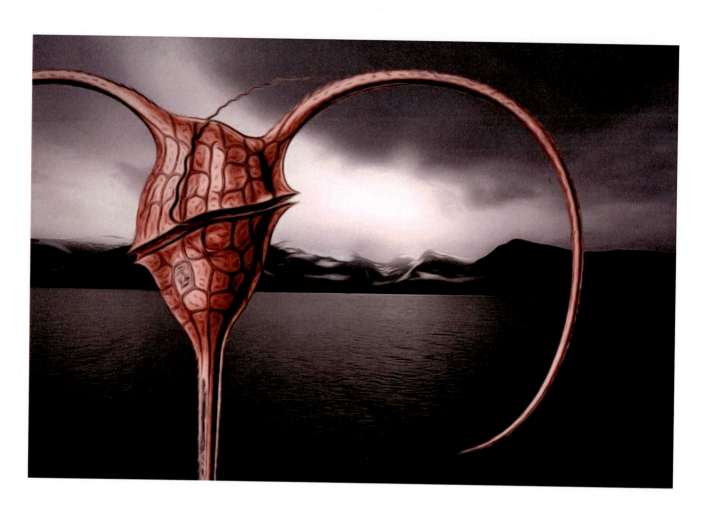

-*Ashley Parker Owens*

withered vines
the tourniquet fails
to raise a vein

sleepless
losing count
of the pills

crows in the trees
darkness swallows
their cries

no moon tonight
I drift between nightmare
and darkness

-Rachel Sutcliffe

Christmas Eve

Each Christmas Eve, Dog Town slows and thickens just a bit more. Clumps of snow come down as if on parachutes. A parasagittal scan would reveal flesh giving way to paper, but paper at least painted to bring to mind precious metals.

You can find me before midnight braving the cold, dropping giftwrapped bones from the slaughterhouse around town. On this holy night, the dogs will have theirs. They will have their say if not. The strays, at midnight, speak, but I would rather hear them gnawing bones. The miracle tarnishes. The animals mostly speak of animal matters: fucking and killing. Our prayers are heard like the nailing of boards.

-*Glen Armstrong*

Freaks

Let me in.
The night is beginning.
To grow fins.
To slowly wreathe from its own.
Arms and legs with a dagger.
Between its teeth.
I need to rethink a few recent.
Choices.
The night is never a single.
Voice always voices.

There's a way of noticing.
To such an extent that noticing.
Becomes destroying.
The eye allows the heart.
To toy with improbable kisses.
There's a way of seeing.
That rips the seen.
From the natural world.
The sun sets and silhouettes.
Soften into shadows.

-Glen Armstrong

ibis headed man
you are crescent moonish...
Thoth waxes poetic

bottomless...
sucked into a sinkhole
of nightmares

day melting
into the icy night...
neptune blues

Fibonacci...
the death spiral
of a hermit crab

-Pat Geyer

She seemed quieter
She acted, spoke, and lived
As if she had something once
That was ripped away from her.
As if she had trusted the world
And opened her heart,
Only to have it stomped on
And thrown back in her face.
As if carrying on was a burden.
She kept giving and giving,
And people kept taking and taking.
And slowly she wasted away
Into a shell of a girl,
Smiling on the outside,
Wondering when someone
Would finally give back to her.

-M. C. T.

-Michael Rehling

-Michael Rehling

language fails...
i think there is a haiku
in that

-Michael Rehling

pixel by pixel
light finds it way
nightsky

-Michael Rehling

ghost writer
tying in the loose ends
of a horror story

full moon
the soundhole abyss
resonates with me

asylum stairs
the blood moon flirting
with a bum

-Roman Lyakhovetsky

rosary beads
the urine smell
under the bridge

recurring nightmare
what I see
in his eyes

the new cuts on her arm hidden report card

-Deborah P Kolodji

The feelings return
The needle punctures my skin
Memories bleed in

-Charlotte Riewestahl

bedrock

dig
deeper until you reach
the bedrock I am made of
drill down beyond
wire nerve
subterranean
tears
down, down
past silent grief
blood magma
excavate
despair

nearly there

now

I am stone.
pain carved me.
safe now.

-Mandy Macdonald

bloodless

i never touched you
not though we lay
together all night twined
like ivy
        how was it your
        knife
        edges
cut me not to the bone?

    *

in the dark of the summer
            stiletto glint

we danced en
        tranced
the blade went in
and drew no blood

the pain is later on
the pain is in looking back

    *

this is gouged out of pain like
a bullet from the flesh
where it has burrowed in
but no
        blood flows

-Mandy Macdonald

-Leslie Bamford

-Leslie Bamford

-Leslie Bamford

Shadowed Truth

tumbleweed
whether to stay or go
or stay

    they gather to read
    her one-page Will

a portrait of her
in a tie-dye dress
flowers in her hair

    sidelong glances –
    a baby too big
    to be preemie?

the hawk's swift descent
as day turns to shadow

    polygraph test –
    how much truth
     is too much?

-Carol Judkins & David Terelinck

The Future is Watching

-Brendan McBreen

Mist Song

Years from now, in a church, a man, bearded as if standing in mist, rosary in hand – furred in salt and smoke, doling out each bead as if it were heartbeat, a man who prays for the man I am now – my life, mist – his muttering, the clack of beads.

Creature Song

Again, my own creature scrabbles overhead. An apocalypse's pulse in every movement. From bed, I cannot see the roof. From bed, I give the creature fur and claws and teeth. From bed, two eyes of ink, and the urgency of one fallen and trying to dig back into the sky.

-José Angel Araguz

The Dragon of Nite Shade

The man road up to the crossroad and looked down the overgrown lane. The old sign was covered with brambles and vines, but could still be read, "Nite Shade". A ripple of heat passed through his chest as he rode on and stopped a few miles up the road. He dismounted and walked around several trees, finding an ancient hidden path that wound up the mountain. The man walked for more than an hour before reaching the ledge that overlooked the burned, blacken valley. Even after more than twenty years, nothing had grown in the dead soil. He sat remembering the past through the prism of time.

The legend grew from century to century, in the small dark village of Nite Shade. It was said that upon All Hollows eve, in the thirteenth year of each new century, they would come. The legend said that for thirteen days, a soul would be taken between moon-rising and moon-setting, until a thirteen-year-old child was given to them for their hideous feast. If no child was given, all would be taken. The old ones told of demons living in the tangled wood just south of the village, where each leaf cut and scarred, and every fruit killed. They were brought to this world by the curse of a witch, burned in the year of our Lord 1613. It was in that fateful year that Terrina was set ablaze for her evil witchery. In her last agonizing breaths, she had forever cursed the people of Nite Shade.

It was the year of 1813 and All Hollows Eve would be upon the village in one more moon-rising. The people of Nite Shade had seen one die for the last eleven nights. At first, it was thought to be unfortunate tragedies, but after the third man was found dead the fear began to grow. He was discovered in front of his own door with the key in the lock and no marks upon his body, his face frozen in terror. As each day passed there was one less in the village and the cries of grief grew.

After the eleventh death, a boy hid from the world in the holiest of places, the church's tall steeple. Telling not even his mother where he veiled in the darkness of god's light. For he had heard the grumbling of the people and felt their fear. They talked of the deaths. They talked of the curses. They talked of the boy with a dragon upon his breast. A sign they said, a sign of death. As the sun rose the twelfth was found. Seth Quill was dead in the street and the people began to search for the one to be given. They looked for the boy with the dragon upon his breast. No other would do, for no other was cursed. House to house and street to street, they searched until they came to the home of the boy with a dragon upon his breast. They pounded upon the door demanding their prey. When those within cried out, "we know not where he lay," the mob grew vengeful and deadly that day. They swung their clubs and waved their torches. In one fateful moment, a torch was thrown and the family within paid with their lives, in an inferno of death. The remorseless mob continued on their way, leaving the dying to their pain.

The bright moon and curiosity was the boy's undoing. He heard the death cries and looked over the edge of the steeple's open belfry, there was his home and family burning at the hands of fear. The moon lit his face, allowing one from the mob to notice him. Soon he was trussed up and carried away. Through the village they dragged the boy of thirteen, all could see, but no one would protect him. He was left upon the ground, at the edge of the dark wood, there to be a sacrifice for a village of fearful fools. The boy shivered in the cool of the night as the ropes scored the soft flesh of his body. He heard the rustling of the tangled woods, and formless shadows began to collect about him.

His chest warmed and burned a bit as the shapes began to form into hideous beasts before his eyes. As his fear rose, the heat within his body grew hotter and hotter, until his whole being seemed on fire. The ropes burnt off and his shirt turned to ash. The dragon image upon his breast moved with each fiery beat of his heart. The dragon began to pull away from his young body. A sudden massive pain paralyzed him as a golden light appeared above. He watched in wonder as a small golden dragon fluttered before his eyes, like some shimmering butterfly of a time long gone. It then slowly circled, growing with each beat of its wings. It grew, and grew until it was a size beyond the boy's comprehension. The great beast then turned to the forms emerging from the darkened wood. A great golden flame came from its mouth, surrounding the boy with a fire that did not burn, but warmed his body and healed his flesh. From beyond the flames, he heard screams of anguish as he slipped into a deep slumber.

When he awoke, the dragon was back upon his breast and the dark wood about him was smoldering ash. He got up and walked toward the village, but all he found were burnt out buildings and death upon the land. He saw a glittering gold spark on the blackened soil. He reached down and picked up a small solid gold cross and he held it to his chest. As he moved to the center of the village only one wall remained upright in the smoldering rubble. It was the white back wall of the church of God, with a single wood cross still hanging upon its remains. The boy could see words of gold, emblazoned below the cross of old.

"ALL EVIL DIES UPON A DRAGON'S BREATH!" The boy read upon the wall of white. He turned away from the sight with tears in his eyes and left the valley of Nite Shade far behind.
The man came out of his memories and stood. He reached into his pocket and took out a small gold cross. He turned from the sight, vowing to never look upon the dead valley again.

-A. D. Adams

I Am Here For You

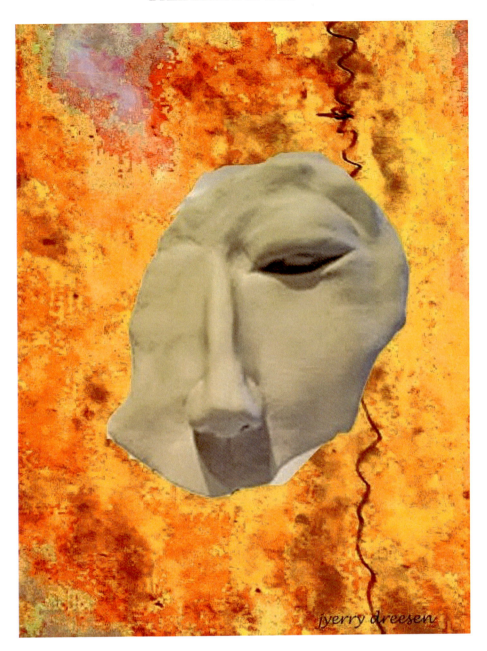

-*Jerry Dreesen*

Give Me One More Drink

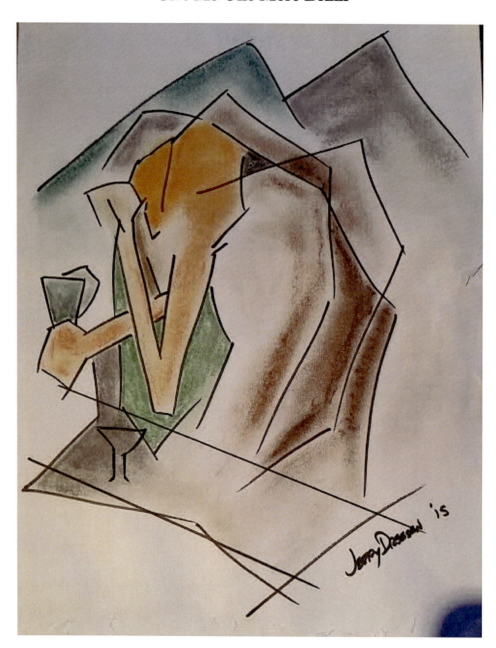

-*Jerry Dreesen*

boiling number 6
in a vat of lye
for three hours
he wonders where he'll put her
once she turns into liquid

their faces
turn from lust to horror to
pure relief –
maybe I won't tell this one
I'm HIV positive

an angel of death
that's what she called herself
when she killed
the only man
who ever loved her

a naked body
found floating in the lake
eyes and lips sewn shut –
the screams of the child
who came to feed the ducks

feeling something's off
I hack his computer for
proof
embedded in the pics of
our baby, child porn

-*Susan Burch*

on her eighth birthday
she found out monsters are real...
innocence lost
in the stench of stale whiskey
and father's cheap cologne

The Hour

she boils the kettle
makes his breakfast, as though it
were a normal day

no words are spoken
he hides behind his paper
to avoid her eyes

she watches the clock
chain-smokes just for something
to do with her hands

she holds back the tears
as the hour hand turns eight
feels her throat tighten

somewhere in a dark prison
their son's body stops twitching

-*Tracy Davidson*

-*Annika Lindok*

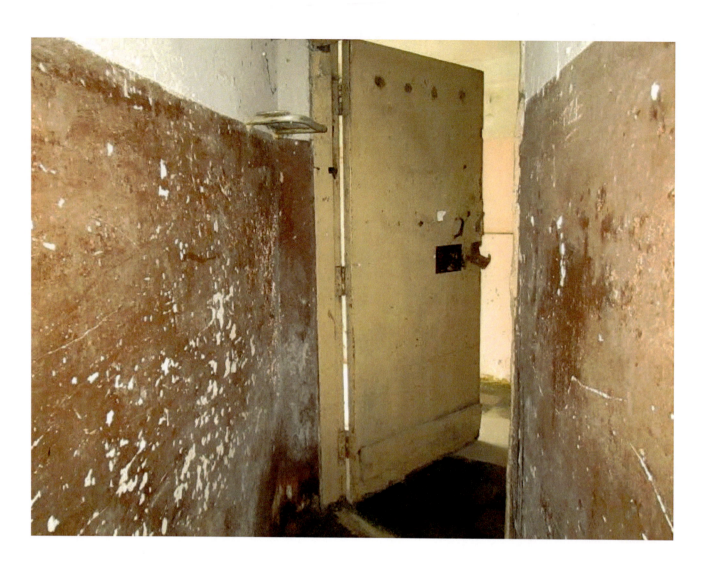

-*Annika Lindok*

Talk at your table
The chains around my body
while i eat your cake

closed in this room-
i could die at this wall
where i shouted for years

-Angelica Costantini-Hartl

psych ward window
a girl's face on grimy glass
talks dirty to me

uncarved pumpkins
grin and giggle
on the dead man's porch

-Tyson West

An Untitled Haibun

The movement on the wall was always the same. A broad sweep disappearing into the corner only to turn and disappear through the wardrobe door
After another cold sweat the duvet would slowly lower off my face to reveal a new bout of darkness

growing up
the disappearing shadows
of head lights

-Robert Kingston

No Stars

Ten-year-old Melinda turned around to look for a sign from the evening sky. The stars are early. Her mother used to whisper close to her ears: Don't be afraid, baby. You will never be alone. Some of us turn to heavenly bodies that shine bright to remind their loved ones that they have not left. Melinda fingered her mother's name inscribed on the grave, just beside her father's. She believed every story her mother told her. It was a quiet afternoon with dark clouds hovering. When the sun has set, she rose and hurried toward the gate of the cemetery where someone older than her mom had been waiting. We are not stars, Aunt Rita. We're no stars. Mom is no star; neither is dad. The so-called Aunt Rita shrugged her shoulders, nodding in agreement. Melinda took a cigarette from Aunt Rita's pocket and lit it. Aunt Rita gasped in disbelief for a moment until Melinda spoke. The stars won't be coming out tonight I believe. She tugged at her Aunt Rita's arm and mumbled her goodbye to her mom and dad.

-Angelo B. Ancheta

The Good News

Apostle's Creed done. Our Father done. Hail Mary done. Glory Be done. The Act of Contrition done. Gabriel made sure that he spent more time than usual meditating on each word of each prayer, the kind of prayer that brings him peace. In just a few minutes, no one will miss "Save the World". He once did it with the unconditional love spam. Everybody picked it up like it was God's plan. But they didn't change. They never could, Gabriel kept thinking.

After one more ejaculatory prayer, Gabriel set the antidote image and finalized the conditions for its effectiveness. The communion will begin with some sort of hallucinogenic effect induced by the multimedia presentation. This time everyone will remember him not only as the Messenger. He knows he could be caught but he is not bothered. Even the highest authority will take the cudgels up for him. He has the approval of all the saints.

A few minutes before 6 pm, he pressed the hotkey. The defrag process only takes a few minutes but to some it will take much longer. The moment they log in to the matrix, the Inception will begin instantly. For now, the fractals and the prelude take over. He prefers doing it with his eyes closed.

-Angelo B. Ancheta

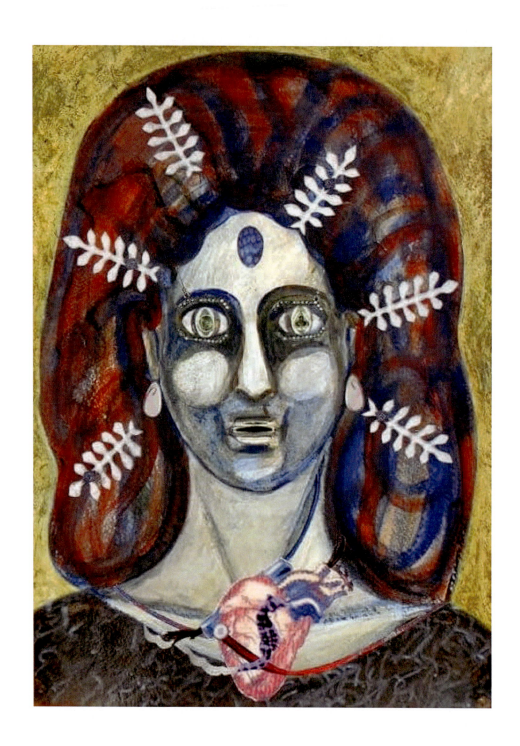

-Toti O'Brien

-Toti O'Brien

-Toti O'Brien

i sang at my grandmother's funeral

like eight measures of intro
all my father's children stood
me and seven siblings, collected to sing
a hymn that must have been her favorite

i have forgotten the title,
the words, the melody and harmony
but still see vividly how i held
forgiveness on the tip of my heart's tongue
ready to unblame brothers for past offenses

song ended, we returned
each to our reserved place
each to our private reservations
almost speaking aloud the whispered pardons
we desperately needed to give
to receive

until hesitation became decision
silence disguised as sorrow
another chance to reconcile
scattered like the sprays of dirt
that clattered on her casket

-Jim Lewis

Walking the Graveyard of My Poems

I hate to see another poem
just go off to die in my great
haunted bleak poetry graveyard,
where my tattered abecedarians
are laid to an early rest.

I hate to feel the pain of bidding adieu.
Goodbye, my diseased haiku,
weak with enjambments,
stilted suffocated syllables
cut off in their prime.

I walk among my dead,
leave flowers for their memory
as collapsed sonnets begin to decay.
I say a rhyming prayer
for twisted sprained forms.

I nod to the skeletons
of overworked metaphors
that have come in couplets to die.
I blow a kiss to the sad
scattered disembodied stanzas.

I loathe to see my poems
hurry home to a mother's love.
Other grave walkers won't
miss my decapitated
little darlings as I do.

I just hate to see another lively
dancing ode pirouette and perish.
I shed a tear and looking
skyward hope my rhymes soar,
and wither nevermore.

-Kathleen A. Lawrence

Shadow Beach

Pterodactyls circle
gray cloak of sky rippling.
Like puppets on a string,
swoop and swing down
as if controlled by some
hidden master pilot
secretly working high
above the shredded clouds.
With each kamikaze dive,
they grab sticky toddlers
from the teeter totter,
jungle gym, and baby slide
like hungry moviegoers
mindlessly snatching
popcorn from a big bucket.

Terrified mothers running
every direction, cover babies
in prams with crocheted
blankets with satin trim,
hurl gravel, purses, shoes,
whatever loose makeshift
grenade they can find.
Diaper bags become bombs,
umbrellas become bayonets,
racing to rescue their darlings
in overalls and eyelet sun hats.
Grasping, so desperate,
neither silky clouds
nor tangerine sunset can break
the moms' myopic charge
to rescue, to save, to love.

Tight in their talons, babies
seem oblivious to danger,
giggling at shiny objects
catching their eyes,
reflecting off the water.
Green-gray warm-blooded
screams above the sea,
smiling at the fish,
sparkly snacks trapped
by shiny conical teeth.

Flying jaws create
squawking shadows
over a real-life ocean mobile
distracting the children
with fitful, angry, salty waves.

Misery laps at the shore and
cries beat against the rocks.
Winds bluffing and snorting
can't deter the singular focus
of the leathery murder birds
to eat, to dine, to chill.

-*Kathleen A. Lawrence*

Air Show

-Roger Leege

Water Shot

-Roger Leege

midnight son

born between two days
at midnight
not knowing who
would take me home

I reach into the dark
for the light
that might reveal
my life

silence hides the truth
in darkness I listen
for a voice

-Bob Bamford

terrified by her
father's drunken rage
she fears me too

-Bob Bamford

another bedtime story same nightmare

-Marion Clarke

Brain Fever

One night I developed an attack of brain fever
I awoke in a sweat

In strange land
far far way
In a Time long ago

All I could see was but my dream
Quietly, slowly,
The dream faded away

Assuming the proportions
Of a dead elephant
Stoned from too many drugs and alcohol.

-Jake Cosmos Aller

Black Vultures

Out of the scurrilous deadly night air
Came like a god damned bat
Out of the fires of hell

That hideous black vultures
Heralding yet another victim to their spell

I arose out of my dope-induced dreams
And alcoholic reveries
And came to an awareness of where I was

And who were these creatures
That were laughing at me

I had done nothing wrong
Except to dare
To be different

Therefore, a communist pinko fagot
By implication if not deed

I cry out
Let us be free

And they reply
With a slanderous lie

That I was not to be
God did not like me at the time

Will he ever
How could a sane god create such as me
And not die laughing

Life is a game
And the winner is those who can remain sane

When out of the scurrilous night air
The vultures come for you

Demons who attempt to steal my Soul
And lock it in a bar
In Cleveland

And then poison my thoughts
With lies about heaven and hell

I just want to live in happiness
Dear God
Is that too much to ask?

Nothing but silence greets me
And the mocking laughter of the

Demonic black vultures
Satan's designated drinkers

-*Jake Cosmos Aller*

Urban Safari

He chisels the invisible again,
a lion's head
slowly taking shape
in the crosshairs of midnight.

In his dreams, it will move
through the tall grass,
lick its paws,
eventually corner him
like a poor man on Wall Street.

I do not ask about the bent Remington
next to the picture of Hemingway
on the wall of his studio,
nor the many bullet holes
in the high ceiling
that breathe like someone
in quicksand.

-Darrell Lindsey

Prayer of Stars

Woods full of dogs with blue eyes,
the blood moon
shining on the young man
in orange garb
with barbed wire wounds
who has stopped
to finger the guard's rosary beads,
catch his breath
that feels like rolling thunder.

Should he reach the river,
perhaps he will drink the prayer of stars
before his life began.

-Darrell Lindsey

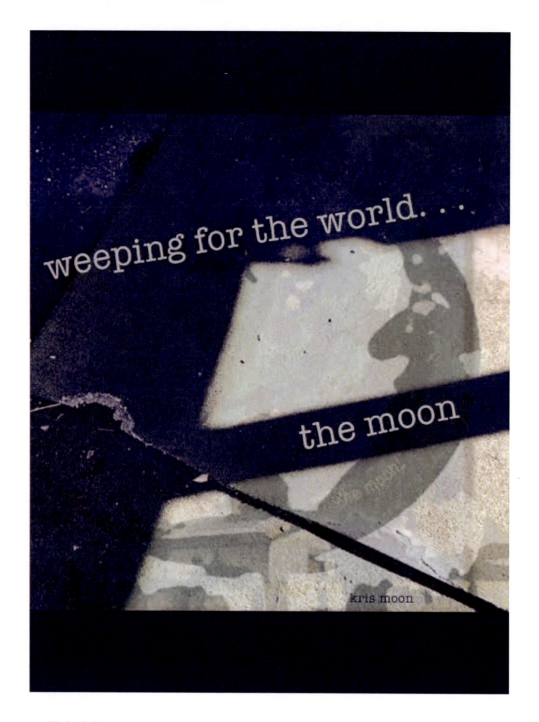

-Kris Moon

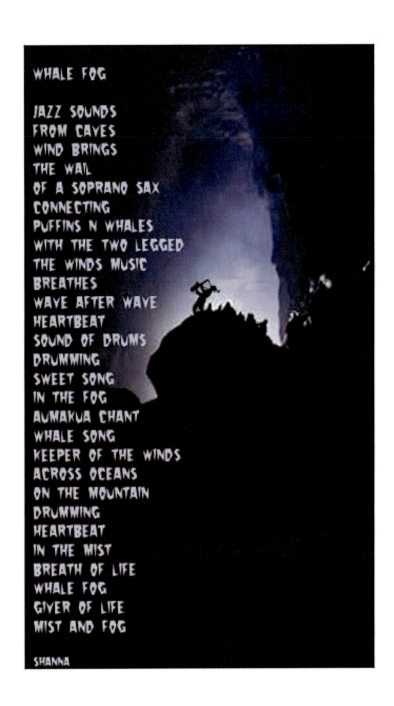

-Shanna Baldwin-Moore

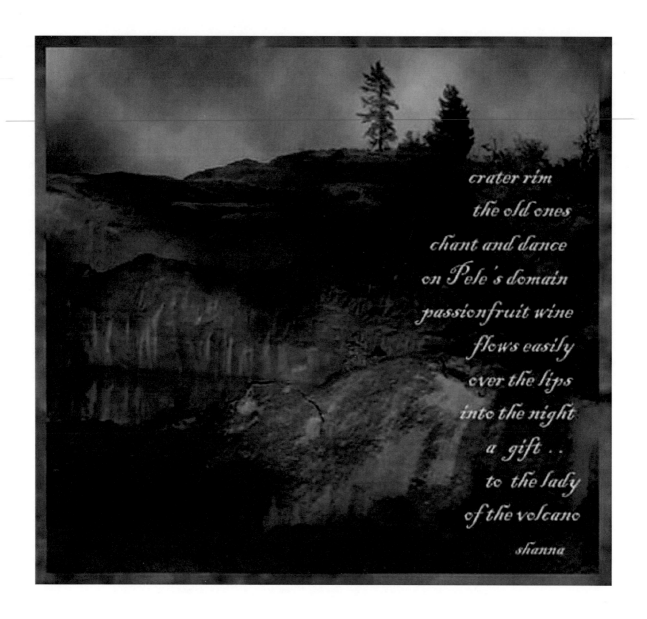

crater rim
the old ones
chant and dance
on Pele's domain
passionfruit wine
flows easily
over the lips
into the night
a gift ..
to the lady
of the volcano

shanna

-Shanna Baldwin-Moore

The young fishermen
bringing home what they've caught
from street hookers.

-RP Verlaine

the persistent
push of time and tide
turning eighty
and you tell me again
of your exit plan

David Terelinck

-David Terelinck

salt in the wound
an early memory
of razor play

-Susan Mallernee

-Susan Mallernee

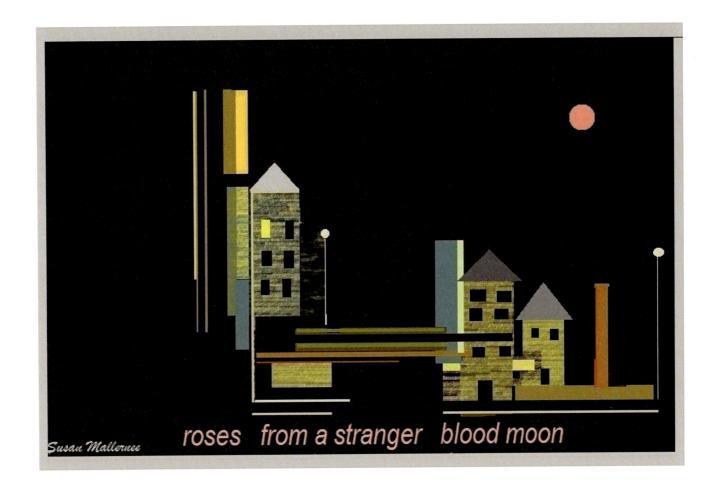

-Susan Mallernee

Sink Hole

God, is that you?
It's me, Steve – at least
I was Steve when I went to sleep.

I gotta coupla questions for you.
First, why me? Did you
finally get really tired of my snoring?

Or did you just get tired
of doodling on big cereal pads
of corn or wheat?

You certainly had us talking
last summer when you got
creative with those intricate circle designs.

Fun, I guess, unless you gotta
subtract the loss of revenue
from all that flattened grain.

You like circles; I get it –
The circle of life, the planets
in orbit around a big ass sun... .

What? You just got bored
and decided to get your big thumb
behind a planet or asteroid Tombolly?

Thought, look, there is Steve, fast asleep.
Do I look like a crystal or cat's eye
you just hadda have for your marble bag?

Did you bull fudge or yell across the cosmos
"Totem poles" and draw a cross
from the perimeter into my little orb?

Didja bull fudge, dude, or just
like callin' the tune that has us
all hummin' and two-steppin' in time?

A sink hole?! Twenty feet across?!
Right under my bedroom? That's rich!
Now you see me; now you don't?

What about my family and friends?
You like watching them scratch their noodles
After all attempts to rescue me failed?

That's kinda sick, innit?
What did I do to tick you off—
Or do you just not give a toss?

Fate?! Whose? Mine or yours?
You're the guy with the stop watch,
not me! Jeez, you run out of criminals?

Couldn't find a few n'er do wells
to take out that fateful night?
What? Am I chopped liver to you?

So now what? Am I a new foot soldier
for your zombie apocalypse when it comes?
Do you have some problem with my coppin' Z's?

Jeez! You know I liked bein' a farmer!
Fillin' America's bread basket and all that...
It's not like I've been suckin' on a hind tit!

It's been a year. You're gonna open up
that sucking maw, again?! Who's next?
How about my wife? Coulda had a life with her.

-*Richard Stevenson*

Airships: The First Wave

Are aliens in control of our species?
Have they been visiting earth for centuries?
Have they been introducing advances in science
and medicine, been advancing our culture
while they've been tinkerin' with our pia mater,
swiping blood and plasma to create hybrid golem?

What happened in 1897? Did some crazy smart
inventor create airships and refuse to get a patent?
Or did aliens create the first of many screen events
to make it look like a whiskered old gent from overseas
was at the helm? Make their saucers appear to be
cigar-shaped zeppelins with ropes and props, and gondolas?

Were leprechauns, fairies, and elves just playful alien imps
trying to create a legend or two to draw us deeper
into myth and magic thinking? Was the star
that led the shepherds to a stable in Bethlehem
really a saucer? Did the alien imps fan coals
that got the immaculate breeze past Mary's knees?

Whazzup with that? Airships pre-date balloons,
zeppelins. Were humans being given a boost
into the age of aviation? Are all the new technologies
and inventions we came up with really gifts
fed to us one at a time through credible science geeks
with thick glasses and cranial RAM implants?

I dunno. But if the Wizard of Oz wants to
scoop me up from some cornfield in Kansas,
I'm game. He doesn't need to grab his wardrobe
from Hollywood costume stores. If he were gonna
mess with my magneto or chromosomes,
I'd prefer he turned up in T-shirt and jeans.

Wanna take a spin around the galaxy
and drop me off on some California dune,
that's cool. If I come in mutterin' from the cold
and hand off some thumb drive or one of our guys
finds some implant in my gourd, that's cool too.
Help yourselves. I won't be packin' stone tablets at least.

Forget Moses. Mose Allison's yer man.

He's got rhythm; he's got soul. And Lord knows
we need it. As he says, let's give God a day off.
He or his minions gave us reason, so we
could use the information properly someday.
Why don't we do it? Give him a day off with pay.

-*Richard Stevenson*

Editorial Review of Elliot Nicely's Haiku Collection *"The Black Between Stars"*

The Black Between Stars is a brief yet elegant collection of haiku by Elliot Nicely. What first drew me in to this little book of poems was the simplistic design of the cover – a blank white consisting of nothing more than the title and the poet's name. The words definitely do all the speaking in this collection. Here's an example.

first prayer
of the wake
only the wine breathes

The Black Between Stars reads like a requiem of poetry that seems to sing along to the quiet melody of the turning page. The subject of grief is rarely handled with such grace, But Elliot Nicely's words resonate with an unfiltered realness that invites us into the most intimate glimpses of mourning in such a way that almost makes us their own.

what would have been
our anniversary
scent of snow

In conclusion, The Black Between Stars is a must have in the library of any haiku enthusiast. I am extremely fortunate that Elliot sent us this wonderful book. I will leave you now with the title poem –

waiting
for her lab results
the black between stars

Editor's Note
If you have a collection of literature and/or art you would like to see reviewed in Scryptic, Please contact us via our website.

Heart of Stone

If you ask most women, they would probably compare themselves to a diamond or pearl... maybe even a ruby. I think women are more attracted to those sorts of gems because they're shiny, beautiful, and expensive. If you ask me, I'd say I'm an onyx. On the outside onyx is dark and mysterious, but their meaning runs much deeper than that. If I remember correctly, onyx is Greek for "claw" and its spiritual use is for cleansing negative energy within yourself and healing sorrow. I feel this applies to me because I continuously claw my way out of depression. I have a dark exterior with a deeper meaning to heal myself from the grief.

heart of stone
the raven escapes
my grasp

-Lori A Minor

Self Portrait

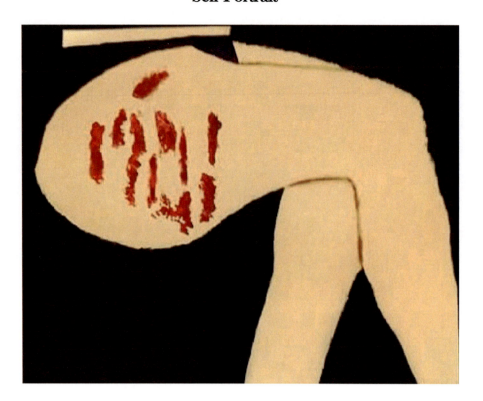

-Lori A Minor

-Lori A Minor

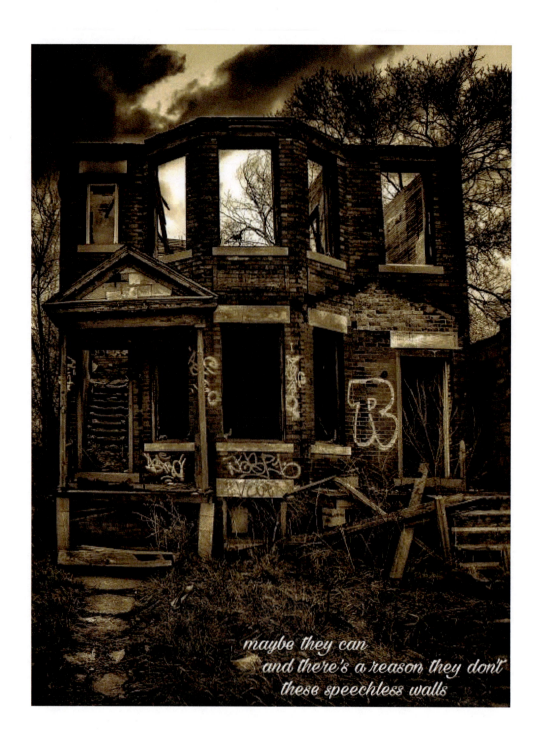

-Chase Gagnon

-Chase Gagnon

Falling Angel

I'm pregnant with Satan's baby but nobody believes me. Those were the first of the few words she said to me, the homeless junkie who I met one morning while sitting in a park near Fisherman's Wharf in San Francisco. She was crying manically and scratching the scabs on her arms; begging for help from tourists, business men, and bleach blondes in sunglasses who all pretended not to see her. Her loneliness was palpable, and I could tell just by looking at her she hadn't slept in days.
I had just spent my first night on the streets after breaking up with my girlfriend, and having spent my last dime on a bus ticket back to Detroit that would leave a few weeks later. Needless to say I was broken. Broken by a kind of pain that nobody in their right mind would question my sanity for. But I could tell her pain was every bit as real as mine, and much deeper.

"Oh really, how far along are you?" I asked in a sympathetic tone. She looked at me for only a second before spacing out when the screech of a passing streetcar dragged her attention away, along the rails and through the fog like a banshee barreling into the maw hell. I've never seen an expression of fear quite like hers - but I watched that flash of of unimaginable horror swell in her eyes, until the tempest slowly crept away from her face as she gradually remembered I was sitting beside her.
She turned her gaze back to me and smiled, with the remnants of tears still glistening in the California sun. I'll never forget the last words she said to me, before wandering back into the arms of her demons - "I can tell you're an angel, because you're the only person who can see me."

ashes taken
away by the wind –
I count my sins
cigarette
by cigarette

-Chase Gagnon

Edited by Chase Gagnon and Lori A Minor, 2017
Cover Photo Credit Lori A Minor

Made in the USA
Middletown, DE
31 October 2017